The Museum of Fresh Starts

poems by

Robin Richstone

Finishing Line Press
Georgetown, Kentucky

The Museum of Fresh Starts

Copyright © 2019 by Robin Richstone
ISBN 978-1-63534-902-3 First Edition
All rights reserved under International and Pan-American Copyright Conventions. No part of this book may be reproduced in any manner whatsoever without written permission from the publisher, except in the case of brief quotations embodied in critical articles and reviews.

ACKNOWLEDGMENTS

"Real Facts" was first published in *Christian Science Monitor*
"The Humboldt Current" and "Spring" in *Cumberland Poetry Review*
The Knitting Project of the Women's Commission for Refugee Women and Children in *Edgz*
"Full Moon" in *Fox Cry*
"The Dove in the Traffic Light" in *Glass Works Anthology*
"The Christmas Story" in *North American Review*
"Old Stories" in *Timber Creek*
"Ordinary Nights" in *Yankee*

Publisher: Leah Maines
Editor: Christen Kincaid
Cover Art: "Whither Shall I Wander," © Rachel Mello, 2009
Author Photo: Douglas O. Richstone
Cover Design: Leah Huete

Printed in the USA on acid-free paper.
Order online: www.finishinglinepress.com
       also available on amazon.com

Author inquiries and mail orders:
Finishing Line Press
P. O. Box 1626
Georgetown, Kentucky 40324
U. S. A.

Table of Contents

The Museum of Fresh Starts 1

The Christmas Story 2

Lebanon, for Andreé 3

The Cats of Baghdad 4

The Knitting Project of the Women's Commission 5

Old World Maps 6

Bethesda, House of Mercy 7

Ordinary Nights 8

El Día de la Raza 9

The Humboldt Current 10

Thirty Degrees South 11

Spring 12

Old Stories 13

The Dove in the Traffic Light 14

On the Road 15

Full Moon 16

Pantoum for a Lost Cat 17

Real Facts 18

The Museum of Fresh Starts

On a claw-marked hillside
in a town called Independence
the Museum of Fresh Starts
holds the wagon ruts and letters
of nineteenth century hope,
archives of a hundred thousand reasons
for leaving things behind,
the world more full of reasons
every day: pioneers, who scattered
those who came before,
be tender to those who come behind
when catastrophe pounds their streets,
burning every house, a hail of stones,
a flight of spears, or guns, or bombers,
drought, famine, when they turn
to make new traces
over your fossil trails
remember your lives as refugees
shouldering through grassland
as have we all since Eden,
tall with our new two-legged stance
that moved the horizon
from the edge of the African plain,
looking into the future,
no way to go back.

The Christmas Story

We know by heart these stories
of a cold world, unwelcoming inn,
the murderous tyrant,
Mary on a donkey, escape,
how cruel, how long ago, how far
from what we mean to sing,
O Come, O Come,
to the weary, the terrified,
Mary's heart beating fast,
her grip on the baby,
the strains of it fill the shops,
the streets, flow down rivers,
cross seas, cross borders,
the refugee mother kneels
to change her infant in
an open field, the shepherds gone,
the angels quiet,
her safety now
completely up to us.

Lebanon, for Andreé

Tough roots hold together
the ineradicable fragrance
of those famous trees,
scent of the bride's garment,
the bridegroom's countenance,
the merchants of Tyre
who furnished Solomon
with temple, chariot, and song,
for twenty thousand measures of wheat,
the fistfuls of prophets
with luxury to condemn,
tongue after tongue licking flames,
a few Phoenician loan-words
studded like stars
in the flowing Arabic night,
and over strange seas of refuge,
that ancient alphabet,
and a dozen towns named
for the cedars,
in the damp American midwest,
north of Goshen,
south of Damascus,
standing up out of the wilderness
like pillars of smoke.

The Cats of Baghdad

> *"A cat, having heard one huge suicide bomb go off,
> tends to take a second one in stride."*
> John Burns, The New York Times

The Fertile Crescent gave rise to domestic cats
as it made us farmers with surplus grain,
at wit's end to preserve our winter stores:
at last Inanna hears our plea, the cat appears,
destroys marauding mice and birds, saves the harvest,
miraculously clean and tidy in her habits,
suitable for our new idea of home.
We set out offerings to keep her near.
After eight or ten thousand years with us,
cats know much about our kindnesses,
our cruelties, and how to shelter
amid these predators' truths: that death
at a distance need not concern us,
or not enough to change the way we live.

The Knitting Project of the Women's Commission for Refugee Women and Children

On rows of cots, the newly homeless women
sit looking into distance
for faces that have disappeared.
Lost rooms keep them awake at night,
stolen flower gardens
numb every movement,
remembered pots and pans
of favorite, ordinary meals
weigh down their shoulders.
They have nothing to do
with their hands.
When the skeins of yarn reach them
they take up the thread;
fiber moves through their fingers,
wraps around the cold, indifferent needles,
and clicks the clockless afternoon
into rows and intervals.
Pattern moves slowly
in with them again.

Old World Maps

> *"Around the turn of the sixteenth century, dragons start to withdraw from the seas west of Europe."*
> *The New Yorker*

They flew to the evangelical dens
of hot-breathed proselytizers. They swam
into anti-evolutionary caves. They slithered
under the flat-earth rocks of the men
who sew the burkas. They took
their backward eyes and love of gold
deep into oil-soaked channels.
They rolled the old maps up in their
armored hearts, remembered, cherished,
in their lairs which are not nests,
because nothing new is raised there.
They laugh at discovery.
However bright the truth that
overwrites them, they bleed through it.
They always come back.

Bethesda, House of Mercy

The lame, the blind, the ravaged,
sigh with bandaged hopes and stumbling heart
because when the angel troubles the water,
only the first one in is healed.
The impure whisper, let me be next,
the devout pray, make me worthy,
the patient saints stay entirely away,
and the visionary sees a flotilla of angels
swooning downward toward the quiet pool,
trouble, trouble, trouble, in their
outstretched, burning hands.

Ordinary Nights

> *"The road to the palace of heaven...is called the
> Milky Way. Along the road stand the palaces of
> the illustrious gods; the common people of the skies live apart,
> on either side."*
> Bulfinch, *The Age of Fable*

The common people of the skies
content themselves with serviceable homes,
building quietly on dark hills
in the suburbs of the galaxy.
After an age or two looking after
cattle, flowers, fruit trees,
childbirth and family hearths,
how good to come home
to a distant view of Cygnus,
leaving Love, War and Wisdom
to those wiser heads
in their bright, quarrelsome houses.

The common people of the skies
are approachable, even to those
who do not know which way
along the road leads to the palace.
Their signs are easy to read
by anyone with half an eye for weather.
Daily they salve
the thoughtless wounds of thunderbolts,
and tend the simple trees
Athena gave.

El Día de la Raza
    (October 12)

On the Day of the People,
the Andean flute is a wind
from the high, cold mountains
to the Quiet Ocean
where fog hangs over
the Humboldt current,
waiting to invade.
On the Day of the People,
the day of five hundred years
of Spanish words, horses in the valleys,
of grapes and wheat,
goats, cheeses, and cattle,
the corn grows,
and the llama walks the passes
under the Southern Cross.
On the Day of
the Braided Strand of the People,
green-eyed women
with long dark hair
teach ancient dances
to children in blue jeans,
they take my hands,
I fall in step,
while the bones of empires
rattle in their graves.

The Humboldt Current

Cold water, a gift from Antarctica,
bounds up the coast of Chile,
its tide of deep-sea fish
feeding centuries of villages,
and eddying the farther rocks
with a cotillion of penguins,
swept so long ago
from their circumpolar home,
grown used to the nearly
equatorial stars
that spatter warm nights
far over their heads,
the sleep of their
long, cool generations
soothed by the chill
that bathes them
in remembered ice,
their history with them,
everywhere they go.

Thirty Degrees South

Scorpio upside down,
Sagittarius way too high,
the struggle for landmarks
takes me half the night.
I have a map, and yet
the Compass, the Square,
the Water Pump, I cannot get.

The Inca serpent
must once have roamed these skies
with Golden Cup,
Stepped Pyramids, Stone Knives,
such secrets
as we can no longer learn,
fallen from grace.

There is no polestar,
yet we turn and turn
around the empty place.

Spring

Today, everyone in the world
gets twelve hours of daytime
and twelve hours of night;
tomorrow we begin again
to steal from each other,
so I've come South, to fill my pockets
where September is March,
a thief in the flowers,
cheating the hemispheres,
like the fork-tailed swallows
in those ruined Mission walls,
you think they're so faithful,
but they want what they can get,
they know that Spring
is anywhere they find it.

Old Stories

Snow paves the horizon
with the ghosts of mountains
that blush in the twilight
watching the back of the sun
cross the equator
and keep going,
drawing the turquoise shadows
into lapis night
that twinkles with fools' gold,
the purse of the prodigal,
spent where winter
will resent it;
then the sun comes back,
sickly, worn, exhausted,
and all the mountains weep
and take it in,
their tears running into the sea,
the sea not filled.

The Dove in the Traffic Light

She has nested in the red light,
a stained glass annunciation:
dove of the traveler. Those who pass
from day to day, from time to time,
journey under the standard, where
the dove waits for her deliverance
while the light comes and goes
and the world stops and starts.

On the Road

These red rocks, once sand,
have been deserted by the sea
more than once, seafloor
with its frozen waves,
incantation from a distant world,
imprint that should have
gone with the tide: not so.
Here it is, perpetual, a wonder.
Tourists come to look at it
from so far away, they cannot understand
each other when they speak.
They hike down into canyons
of ancient incident
and say they will always remember this,
and they hike back up,
and they forget.

Pantoum For a Lost Cat
—for Lucia

You call her but she does not come,
empty bed and ghostly bowl,
the mouse creeps out to steal a crumb,
phantom footsteps on patrol,

empty bed and ghostly bowl
add her absence to the air,
phantom footsteps on patrol,
you've been looking everywhere,

add her absence to the air,
day is gone and night is late,
you've been looking everywhere,
attic passage, garden gate,

day is gone and night is late,
moonlight on a half-seen shape,
attic passage, garden gate,
she was safe, but she escaped,

moonlight on a half-seen shape,
the mouse creeps out to steal a crumb,
she was safe, but she escaped.
You call her but she does not come.

Full Moon

This is the smaller daylight.
Blood goes out of the landscape;
white things glow.
This is the light
that half the stars survive,
the gossip of distant morning,
its shadows clean as noon.
This is the light eclipsed by habitation,
a coin in the cities,
but every transaction of the rural night.
This is the light maligned for changeability,
into whose forgiving face we can look,
and still look again.

Real Facts

> *"A pigeon's feathers are heavier than its bones."*
> —*printed inside a Snapple cap*

Hollow bones support the simple weight
of life toeing a plaza full of crumbs.
The pigeon dips its head to consecrate
my offerings, and the small park becomes
a minor metaphor of good and grace:
what is this bird to me, that I should feed it?
And yet because we share this common place
it brings a kind of kinship, and I need it.
Fueled now, it shakes its heavy wings
and leaps into the air which parts, receiving
the pigeon into more celestial things,
and me into the prospect of believing
that burdens may have usefulness unknown.
Spread, wings, and lift me up to see my own.

Robin Richstone is a writer, painter, and gardener who lived in California, where she edited *The Altadena Review*, and now lives in Ann Arbor Michigan, where she has much more space to garden. Her regular trips to the Chilean desert over the course of ten years provided much subject matter for her paintings and poetry.

Robin has published poems in *Poetry, Borderlands, Briar Cliff Review, Christian Science Monitor, Hawaii Pacific Review, Journal of the American Medical Association, Kansas Quarterly, Kenyon Review, New England Review, North American Review, Santa Barbara Review, Seneca Review, Sycamore, Wild Goose Poetry Review*, and other magazines, many under her previous name of Robin Shectman. Believing that words have power, she changed her name when she remarried.

She writes a gardening blog, which along with some of her poems and paintings can be found at https://robinrichstone.wordpress.com.

www.ingramcontent.com/pod-product-compliance
Lightning Source LLC
LaVergne TN
LVHW041525070426
835507LV00013B/1837